SOUL-WINNING HELPS

For Members of the Healing Professions

Marjorie V. Gray, RN

PACIFIC PRESS PUBLISHING ASSOCIATION

Mountain View, California   Omaha, Nebraska

Oshawa, Ontario

DEDICATION

To all the messengers who go out with
the Book to kindle a light in hearts that
can be reached no other way.

Cover and book design / Lauren Smith
Cover photo / Duane Tank

Copyright © 1975 by
Pacific Press Publishing Association
Litho in United States of America
All Rights Reserved

Library of Congress Catalog Card No. 75-18268

CONTENTS

Star for a Student Nurse 5

How It Came About 8

Getting Started 12

And Now the Book 17

The Need Comes First 20

Meeting Resistance 22

When Time Runs Out 27

Suicide or Christ 30

And Then the Harvest 33

Helps for Soul Winners 35

Why I Wrote the Book

When you are asked to make a book out of an experience very close to your heart—well, you write the book.

So far as I know, I was the first nurse ever hired to devote full time to visiting and Bible studies. Since there were no existing materials prepared for this specific type of witnessing, we could only experiment. Some ideas didn't work. Some did. You might. say we were playing it by ear. I would prefer to say that we were taking a step at a time and letting the Lord lead. He did lead. And He did bless. Of that I am certain.

In the pages that follow I have told something of the background of my work—how it came about and how it developed into a priceless experience. I have shared something of the approach we used, how we found the interest and cultivated it. And what we found in the harvest.

If doctors, nurses, or student nurses can gain some inspiration from what I have recounted, or find it helpful in their witnessing for Christ, I will be tremendously grateful for this opportunity to share.

Marjorie V. Gray, RN

Star for a Student Nurse

It was a late summer evening in 1950. Little did I know, when the phone rang, that it was the beginning of a story—and that I was about to be made unforgettably aware of the impact of our medical ministry upon the lives of patients.

A lady's voice asked for the pastor of the Seventh-day Adventist church. When Don, my husband, took over, she asked that he come to her home because she wanted to become a Seventh-day Adventist. Pastors don't often receive calls like that, and of course Don made an appointment for the next evening.

When Don arrived at the home, he was greeted by the husband and ushered into the living room. There, on a hospital bed, was Jill, evidently a very ill woman. And by only one glance at the hard lines in her face one might guess that hers had been a sinful life.

"Tell me," Don asked, "why do you want to become a Seventh-day Adventist?"

Jill replied, "Because of a little Canadian student nurse who took care of me at the Portland Sanitarium."

Then the thrilling story began to unfold, punctuated by rough army language mingled with cursing. These were so much a part of her that she didn't realize how they must sound to others. She had been an officer in the army during World War II—an efficient and demanding officer I am sure, perhaps an intolerant one. Following her discharge from the

5

army she had married and moved into our community where her husband was in business.

When she became ill, she was referred to Dr. Holden, a surgeon at the Portland Sanitarium. Exploratory surgery revealed that the cancer was too extensive for any remedial action. The surgeons could only close the incision.

As soon as Jill recovered from anesthesia, she became very demanding and abusive. Her language was crude and obscene and, according to the nurses, enough to make a sailor blush. They dreaded to enter her room because of the tongue-lashings they learned to expect. I was told that when her light went on they would find something important to do elsewhere. Sound familiar?

But there was one little student nurse who seemed oblivious to all the mistreatment and obscene language. Every evening she would care for Jill tenderly and patiently. Before she left her room in the evening, she would fluff her pillows and say kindly, "I know what terrible pain you must be in and what a difficult day you have had. I'd love to just ask God to give you relief from this pain and give you a good night's rest."

Then she would bow her head and make that simple request.

Day after miserable day that little student nurse patiently and lovingly cared for this hardened, unkind, former army officer. And Jill never forgot it. She told Don, "Not *once* did that little student nurse become impatient or unkind with me through all that abuse that I gave her." And she added, "You know, pastor, that did something to me inside. I couldn't get it out of my mind. I thought, If that is what a Seventh-day Adventist is, then I want to be one!"

What a testimony!

Don studied with Jill and her husband and spent many hours teaching them God's truth for this hour. He knew that Jill's time was slipping away. How thrilled they were to learn of Christ's love and forgiveness, of heaven and the future life, of God's day of rest, and of Christ's soon coming! How it touched their hearts! There was no problem with smoking or drinking. They loved their Lord so much that His wishes were a pleasure to carry out.

It was not long until they were both baptized, though for Jill her bathtub had to be her baptistery. She was happy beyond words.

And then on a clear, cold day—October 29, 1950—Don conducted her funeral. It was the first military funeral ever held for a woman in our community. But I wasn't thinking of the honor accorded her. As I stood by her grave, listening to the mournful bugle, I was chilled by the thought of what a sad day it would have been except for that student nurse!

I don't know who that student nurse is. Probably she doesn't know that the story had a happy ending—all because of her. Wherever she is, she isn't a student anymore of course. I hope that she may pick up this little book and learn what happened. If not, how exciting it will be for her to hear the story from Jill herself in the new earth!

Ellen White wrote, "Many can be reached only through acts of disinterested kindness. Their physical wants must first be relieved. As they see evidence of our unselfish love, it will be easier for them to believe in the love of Christ. Missionary nurses are best qualified for this work."—*Counsels on Health,* p. 391.

There will be at least one star in the crown of a certain student nurse. How many will there be in mine?

How It Came About

Jill's story was still fresh in my mind twenty years later when I was approached, in December of 1970, by George Pifer, business manager of the East Rose Medical Clinic. He asked a startling question. Would I be willing to terminate my present nursing job and connect with the clinic as a combination of visiting nurse and Bible instructor?

The clinic is located in the southeast section of Portland, Oregon, and five doctors practice there. They are Drs. Howard I. Osborne, Herbert R. Gray, J. Stewart Lloyd, Frederick A. Mote, and C. I. Clifton. Even the five doctors can scarcely care for their large practice. Waiting rooms and parking lots are nearly always overflowing.

At that time the doctors were increasingly burdened about the spiritual needs of their patients. They were so rushed as they attempted to care for the immediate physical problems that there was little time to share their faith and witness for Christ. Often patients would ask questions about our beliefs, their interest initiated by books they had picked up from the bookrack. But there was little time for discussion. The doctors felt the need for someone to spend time unhurriedly with those who had asked questions and with those who were going through traumatic experiences.

When the doctors discussed their problem with the conference administrators, my name was mentioned. It was felt that it would be an advantage to have a registered nurse join the health team for this work, rather than someone not medically oriented.

When George phoned for my answer, I was hesitant. I couldn't help feeling a response to the need and the challenge. But I felt unqualified. I had never been either a visiting nurse or a Bible instructor.

When I voiced my concern about qualifications, I was assured that the role of visiting nurse was one I would fit into quite naturally. And they felt it was just as well that I was not a professional Bible instructor. They wanted to approach the patients from a medical standpoint, win their confidence on that basis, and then lead them to Christ. I would call on the patients simply as the visiting nurse from the clinic. This would be our entering wedge just as the Lord has told us it should be. And how can we fail if we follow His plan?

I was delighted to work in this capacity—particularly because I had felt for some time that I was not being the witness for Christ that I wanted to be. I had attended several witnessing programs and felt a great burden to witness for Christ personally.

It is true that I had been a minister's wife for twenty-three years and had visited along with my husband and helped in his evangelistic meetings. But I felt I had only been helping Don to wintess—not witnessing myself. I had never worked on a one-to-one basis and felt the joy and satisfaction of personally leading souls to Christ. I felt this need in my life.

As a nurse, of course, I had done what I could to make patients comfortable and give them the emotional support they needed. But there was really little time to witness. A hurried word of prayer here and there—yes. But I wanted to do more. I wanted to know some of the satisfaction that Don and many others were experiencing.

So that is how it came about. I began my work at the clinic on January 4, 1971.

As far as we know, this was an untried facet of evangelism in the medical field. There were no materials prepared specifically for such a program. We could only experiment. The methods that proved suitable and brought results we kept. The ideas that proved impractical or worthless we discarded. During the first two months we used the trial-and-error method and sought counsel from God continually. Things seemed to fall into place near the end of the second month. The physicians were so busy that they left the decisions regarding my work largely up to me, knowing that my husband, who was in charge of evangelism for the conference, would give me good counsel.

At the beginning I was given the names of all the patients the doctors felt were interested in the Bible or in our beliefs. I recorded these names on four-by-six cards and slipped them into a six-by-nine notebook in alphabetical order. Then I went to the patients' charts for their addresses, phone numbers, religious background, diagnosis, and prognosis. This information enabled me to visit with the patients intelligently.

Next I arranged the names in a notebook according to districts in the city. This gave me a system whereby I could go quickly from home to home within the one area.

From the doctors' reading rack I made up a box of small booklets on subjects that were devotional or inspirational in character. These I kept in the car, with always a few in my purse ready for immediate use. Later, of course, when I began actually studying with the patients, my box of books covered all our doctrines and beliefs.

The doctors supplied me with a sphygmomanometer, stethoscope, a thermometer, and supplies for injections—even balloons for the children!

I was ready. I was excited. I was apprehensive.

Getting Started

That first day! It was a thrilling yet frightening experience. I prayed a long time before I left home that morning. And I don't think I ever quit praying all day. I learned what it meant to "pray without ceasing." In fact, what else can you do when you feel helpless and frightened?

I had never met the people I would be visiting that day. I didn't know their real feelings. How would they react? Would they be friendly or hostile? Were they individuals who could be interested in the study of the Bible? Would the Lord make an opening so that I could witness for Him? And if He did, would I recognize it? All this was running through my mind.

It was some time later that I found this quotation. I wish I had had it then. "It is not the capabilities you now possess or ever will have that will give you success. *It is that which the Lord can do for you.* We need to have far less confidence in what man can do, and far more confidence in what God can do for every believing soul. He longs to have you reach after Him by faith. He longs to have you *expect great things from Him.* He longs to give you understanding in temporal as well as in spiritual matters. He can sharpen the intellect. He can give tact and skill. *Put your talents into the work, ask God for wisdom, and it will be given you."—Christ's Object Lessons,* p. 146.

While I was in the homes I kept praying silently for openings to witness and for words—just the right words—to say. And you know, the Lord never failed me! Not once!

I used to marvel when my husband preached about the famous George Müller and how he had a little black book in which he wrote down his prayer requests and later the date on which they were answered. It is said that he had fifty thousand prayers answered, with five thousand answered on the very day he made the request. It was hard to believe, really. But it isn't anymore. I wish that I had kept a little black book during the months that I worked for the clinic. I'm sure I could give you some encouraging statistics right here.

Our problem is that we ask and receive. Then we forget and fail even to thank the Lord. We take so much for granted.

Time after time God answered my prayer and made an opening in the conversation where it was easy and natural to bring up the subject of Bible study. It was not difficult or awkward at all to ask people if they had ever studied the Bible systematically. If not, would they enjoy doing so? I would tell them that we had study guides and Bibles at the clinic if they were interested. It was so easy, so perfectly natural, with the right opening. The Lord made the openings. All I had to do was step in. I didn't work alone.

"In this work all the angels of heaven are ready to co-operate. All the resources of heaven are at the command of those who are seeking to save the lost. Angels will help you reach the most careless and the most hardened."—*Christ's Object Lessons,* p. 197.

"Remember that the Lord Jesus is the Master Worker. He waters the seed sown. *He puts into your minds words that will reach hearts."—Testimonies,* Vol. 9, p. 41.

That first day I greeted the people with "Good morning! I'm Marge Gray, the visiting nurse from East Rose Medical

Clinic. Dr. Osborne [or whoever was their doctor] asked me to drop by sometime when I was in this area, just to get acquainted and see how things are going."

Of course, if I needed to give them an injection, take their blood pressure, change a dressing—or whatever it might be—I would give that as my reason for being there.

This first visit was just a get-acquainted visit. We discussed their health problems, how they were feeling, and I jotted down in a little notebook any messages they wanted to send to the clinic or to their doctor. We talked about their families, their work, or whatever was on their heart. I made the visit short, usually just a few minutes. As I got to the door, ready to leave, I would turn and say casually, "Oh, by the way, I brought you a little booklet from the clinic reading rack. I thought you might enjoy it." I always kept the little booklets in my purse and out of sight until the moment they were needed.

Even that first day convinced me that probably no one is more cordially welcomed in the home than the visiting nurse—unless it would be the doctor himself. The doors swung open wide, and I was warmly received. The people were simply delighted that their doctor thought enough of them to send his visiting nurse to call and find out how they were doing and if there were any problems I could help with. Time and again they would remark how wonderful it was that their doctor would provide such a service and without charge. Many were deeply touched by this gesture. Hearts were softened, and barriers broke down.

The one thing that impressed me most that first day is that there are so many lonely people living all around us without our ever knowing it. Some of them were eager to study the

Bible with me. And I knew it was partly because they were so lonely. Lonely people especially need the Saviour. Of course we all need Him, but lonely people seem more aware of their need.

Every week I called on all those who displayed any sign of interest in religion or in the literature I was leaving. If I found no interest at all, I would space the calls farther apart and concentrate on those who showed some interest.

I worked the same way with patients from the clinic who were hospitalized. The doctors usually gave me the names of those who were to have surgery, those who were critically ill, those who had attempted suicide, or those who were having family problems or some other difficulty. I tried to visit these patients at a time when they were alone, avoiding the visiting hours. I told them that I was the visiting nurse and that their doctor had asked me to come by and see how they were getting along and if there was any way we could help.

Often I would use a little humor, if it seemed appropriate, to break the ice. Then I would ask how they were feeling and perhaps about their family. If they were to have surgery and seemed frightened or apprehensive, I would give them the opportunity to express their feelings. I tried to give them some emotional support as well as spiritual. Before leaving these hospital patients I would casually say, "I have to run, but I'd love to have just a word of prayer with you before I leave. I want to ask the Lord to give you a good night and help you get well soon."

The prayer was usually only a sentence or two. Then I would leave a little booklet on prayer or faith or Christ's love. The calls were usually only three or four minutes. But nearly every patient would squeeze my hand and thank me for praying for them. When people are ill, they feel a need that they may not be conscious of at any other time. It is an excellent opportunity to gain their confidence and leave short articles or booklets for them to read.

Physicians with their bookracks, all across the land, are doing a tremendous missionary work, the results of which only eternity will reveal. Our own patients sent booklets all over the United States from the bookrack at East Rose. Twenty-one of these people wrote in to ask for Bible studies. Won't it be a wonderful day when we learn all the results of this literature ministry?

In the back of each booklet on the rack we placed a return postcard so that the reader could mail it back to request Bible studies and a free Bible. It was about five weeks before we got any response. But then the cards began to come in, one or two each week. Several of these patients were baptized while I was at the clinic.

I wonder if we really understand the evangelistic potential when the health approach and the Bible and our literature are used hand in hand!

And Now the Book

During the first two months I had very few actual Bible studies in progress. We searched then for some way to augment our requests. We printed a letter on clinic stationery, giving the patients the opportunity to request a free Bible and study guides if they desired. A sample of this letter is included with the materials in the back of this book.

We intended to send this letter to every patient in our files. But we never got past the first hundred. I just hope no one misses the kingdom because of a name beginning with T or W! The response was overwhelming. With the requests coming back from this letter, and from the bookrack, I was soon studying with sixty people. We were absolutely thrilled. God was really opening doors!

I used the method of Bible study that is outlined in the back of this book. It is simple and effective. Not being a Bible instructor, and not having too good a memory for texts when under pressure, I devised a method that worked very well for me and enabled me to find texts on most any subject quickly and easily. It also made it possible for me to give a study on any of our beliefs without any advance notice.

This is what I did. I purchased a six-by-nine notebook and then secured several sets of Bible lessons—"The Bible Speaks," regular; "The Bible Speaks," advanced; "Revelation"; "Daniel and Revelation"; "The Bible Speaks," youth set; "Christ Speaks to Modern Man"; etc. I also purchased a set of Bible

17

lessons authored by Mary Walsh and called "Doctrinal Bible Studies for the Layman."

Then I took a copy of *Bible Readings* and went over each subject that was covered in the lessons, writing in the answers on my lesson sheets, with additional texts or thoughts between the questions or on the back. I punched the lessons and inserted them in the notebook. I finally ended up with two notebooks of lessons, with the "Revelation" lessons and the "Daniel and Revelation" lessons in a separate notebook.

If, while studying with a patient, I was asked for a text that I could not quickly find, I would say that I would look it up and bring it the next week. At home I would look it up and write it into the lesson so I would have it the next time. This did not happen very often however. Usually I had every text I needed. The advantage of being a visiting nurse rather than a Bible instructor was that people didn't expect me to know all the answers. I was doing the lessons and learning along with them. And the patients liked that.

I always carried a small Bible in my purse. On the flyleaf I listed texts for special needs—forgiveness, heaven, the love of God, help for the bereaved, texts for those having financial problems or other difficulties, etc. These proved very helpful. You will find them listed in the back of this book.

Literature was used freely in my visiting and along with my Bible studies. If I felt the student did not really comprehend a subject, I would leave a booklet for additional reading. However, I did find several people who did not enjoy reading. With these I had to spend much more time in going over each detail of the lesson to be sure it was understood. This is a more difficult type of Bible study to give and uses up a lot of precious time. It is so much better, if you possibly can, to keep the person reading along with the lessons. These individuals will have a much more solid foundation than those who will not read or who want you to read for them.

The patients were learning. And so was I.

The Need Comes First

When I arrived at a patient's home, I found it helpful to give the patient time to talk about anything that might be of concern. In this way I was able to avoid the interruptions that would otherwise come during the study. Once we start the study, I try to keep on the subject. If patients bring up some other topic, I tell them we will soon be having a lesson on that and that they will understand it better if they wait. If you scatter your shots, you won't hit the target.

One day another nurse accompanied me for a study. After we left, she said, "Do you always have to listen to all that stuff about aches and pains and neighbors next door every time you visit?" I said, "Well, yes, I suppose I do." And she shook her head. "That would drive me crazy!"

She had missed the point completely. I was not there to meet my needs. I was there to meet the patient's needs. This was our door to the heart. This particular patient was an elderly widow who lived alone and seldom had company. She needed someone to share her thoughts with. True, it took an extra ten or fifteen minutes. But what will that mean in eternity?

This lady had a very sharp mind and was a diligent student. She had read her Bible through every year for forty-five years. When we studied about the Sabbath, she was amazed. She said, "Think of it! I've read my Bible through forty-five times, and not once did it occur to me that the Sabbath is Saturday.

Saturday *is* the seventh day of the week, not Sunday." She was soon baptized and was happy in finding the true church.

This lady suffered a severe illness and died a few months ago. How happy I am that I took the time to listen! It's a pretty small investment if it means a soul in the kingdom.

The need must come first. That's the path to the heart.

Meeting Resistance

Since those with whom I studied were all patients at the clinic, I was especially careful not to antagonize or offend anyone by pressing a controversial belief too soon. I would like to illustrate the importance of this caution by recounting the experience I had with two of our patients.

Sally had been born and raised in Missouri but was now a seasoned elementary school teacher in Portland. Her quick wit and twinkling eyes were always a source of delight to me. However, she could be stern and severe and precise in her discipline at school. In fact, she half-amusedly told me that her pupils called her "Killer Miller" because she didn't allow any hanky-panky in her room.

I first met Sally in the hospital a few days after she had suffered a severe heart attack. I introduced myself as the visiting nurse from the clinic and told her that her doctor had sent me to see how she was doing. She had been peering at me over the top of her glasses. But when I mentioned where I was from and who had sent me, a quick smile curled her lips and her eyes twinkled. She said, "Honey, if you're a nurse from East Rose Clinic, I'm delighted to make your acquaintance. I'll tell you, I'm alive today because I went to that clinic and found a good doctor!"

The barriers were down. The doctor had opened the way. It happened all the time. Patients have tremendous confidence in Christian doctors. In fact, it almost borders on worship. What an opportunity our doctors have to open hearts to our message!

After Sally left the hospital, I visited her each week at her home, checking her blood pressure, giving injections, and listening to her heart. Each week I would leave something from the bookrack for her to read. We had mailed her one of the letters offering the free Bible and study guides, but she never returned the card or mentioned it to me. I was afraid she was just not interested in spiritual things.

Finally I felt I just must know what her reaction to the letter had been. I prayed for an opening. And then one day as I was caring for her needs, I was impressed to say, "Oh, by the way, Sally, did you get one of the letters from the clinic offering the free Bible and study guides?"

Without hesitation she answered, "Yes, I did. But I didn't want the doctors to think I just wanted a free Bible. Couldn't I get the guides without the Bible?"

"Yes, of course," I told her. "But the guides give the page numbers in that particular Bible. That way you can look up the scriptures by the page number, and it makes it a lot easier."

She said, "Oh, that would be good since I don't know the Bible very well. I'll have to find that card now and send it in."

Of course I told her it wouldn't be necessary to send in the card and that I would run out to the car and get a Bible and a set of guides. (I always kept a box of Bibles and a box of assorted Bible lessons in the trunk.)

As I hurried down the steps to go to my car, I thought of her husband. I had really not become acquainted with him. He was a big man with a deep, gruff voice. I felt impressed that I should bring in two Bibles and two sets of lessons. I did. But I was afraid to ask him if he'd like to study too. I breathed a prayer for courage, and then, after handing Sally's to her, I said, "What about your husband, Sally? Would he enjoy doing the lessons along with you?"

She called him from the next room and explained about the lessons. I said, "Wouldn't you like to study the guides along with Sally?"

"Well, I guess I could do them too."

I was so excited that I could hardly believe my ears. What an answer to prayer!

They were both excellent students, rarely missing a point. Once in a while Gene would get an answer right that Sally missed. This pleased him immensely, since his wife was a teacher.

We studied three lessons a week, going over them carefully and discussing any questions they had. But I was not sure just how deep their interest was. Was it strong enough to make any real changes in their lives?

Whenever we discussed a controversial subject, if I found them resisting, I would back off and change directions. I never argued or pushed. I might smile or chuckle. But I never would become defensive.

When we came to the standards of the church, Sally said quite abruptly, "Well, I'll tell you something, Marge. If I have to quit wearing my jewelry and makeup to become a Seventh-day Adventist, I want you to know I'll never become a Seventh-day Adventist! I've got a neck as long as a Missouri mule, and I feel naked without my necklaces and earrings!"

I detected a note of real resistance and was afraid she would want to discontinue the studies right there. But I asked the Lord silently to tell me what to say. And He didn't fail me.

"Sally," I said, "there are a lot of things that are more important than jewelry and makeup. When you really learn to know the Lord and really love Him, some of these things won't seem so important."

"Well, I'll never take off my jewelry and makeup!"

I smiled and turned to the next lesson and never discussed it with her again.

Many weeks went by. We had finished one set of lessons and then another. And we were halfway through the "Daniel and Revelation" set. One day as I knocked at the Millers' door, I had a real surprise. Sally came to the door pale as a ghost, without a piece of jewelry. I didn't know if she had just crawled out of the shower or if she had intended to look that way. So I was afraid to comment.

I tried not to register any surprise at all. But I noticed as we were studying that Gene kept looking at me and then at Sally. Finally, as we were finishing, Sally jumped to her feet and said, "Well, Marge, didn't you even notice anything different today?"

I still wasn't sure if she had really meant to look that way. So I said, "What, Sally?"

"My lipstick is gone, my jewelry is all gone!"

"I noticed that," I said, now free to show my excitement. "You rascal! You never said one word!"

Then she made an interesting remark. She said, "You know, a long time ago you said that all these things weren't that important when you really love the Lord. And it's true!"

We have to give the Holy Spirit time to work. When we go bulldozing ahead of Him, we lose interests and ruin our chances of winning people for the kingdom. We should be careful not to press for an answer on a controversial belief until we are quite certain the answer will be Yes. When the heart has been softened by the Holy Spirit, these other things will fall into place. There will be no resistance when the life has been completely surrendered to Christ. As people continue to study, the Holy Spirit continues to work. So I always tried to keep them studying. Some individuals had finished seven or eight sets of lessons before they found Christ and were willing to let Him have His way in their lives.

In the back of this book you will find some helpful material on how to lead a person to decision for Christ.

But back to Sally and Gene. They were both baptized and are now happy dedicated Christians. Sally told me, "I'm so glad you didn't push me. You didn't try to force your beliefs on me. It was up to me to make my own decisions."

When Time Runs Out

For several of the patients I visited in the hospital, time was running out. Some had never made the decision for Christ. But at least I could invite them now to accept Him.

Trying to help the dying was probably the most difficult task I faced in my work with the clinic. The responsibility seemed too much for me. It is a solemn thought that a person's final destiny could be influenced by what you say or don't say. And sometimes we don't know in this life whether we have succeeded or not. But the Lord's servant wrote, "This is not a question for us to settle. We are to do our work, and *leave the results with God."—Christ's Object Lessons,* p. 65.

For several months I had visited a lady with terminal cancer. When she was admitted to the hospital for the last time, I felt I must try somehow to help her accept Christ. I had left literature with her on many occasions. She said she had read some of the booklets but not many. She asked for studies, but then she had many excuses and never would follow through. She seemed to want to do what was right, but there was some barrier. She said she knew that our teachings were right and that if she ever joined a church it would be the Adventist Church. But something was holding her back.

Now, as I watched her getting weaker and thinner, I felt I couldn't wait longer. I had to try to reach her. I asked God for wisdom. Then as I walked into her room, I was impressed to take out my little Bible and read to her. I said, "Phyllis, would

27

you like me to read a little from the Bible?"

She responded, "Oh, yes, I'd love that."

So I read about heaven. All the beauties—no sickness—no sorrow—no crying—no death. Then I said, "Phyllis, wouldn't you like to have Jesus reserve you one of those mansions in heaven?"

"Yes, that would be wonderful. But I can't make it."

"Why do you say that?"

"He wouldn't want me. I've done too many things—too many. I've been too awful!"

Here was the answer. She wanted to come to Christ. But when she tried to find Him, the enemy piled all her sins up before her, and she became discouraged. She felt it was hopeless.

I turned to the flyleaf of my Bible where I had the texts for special needs written down and began to read about God's forgiveness. I read many of the precious promises: "If we confess our sins, he is faithful and just to forgive us our sins." "Though your sins be as scarlet, they shall be as white as snow." "He delighteth in mercy. . . . He will have compassion." "He will abundantly pardon."

Then I pointed out that many of God's children in Bible times committed terrible sins. But when they confessed those sins and repented, God forgave their sins and even forgot them. "I will remember their sin no more." I told her these things were in the Bible to give us hope and courage so that we could know that He would freely forgive us too.

I said, "Wouldn't you like to ask Jesus right now to forgive all those sins of the past? Wouldn't you like to just tell Him how sorry you are and how much you want to accept Him and have a home in the new earth with Him?"

Tears were streaming down her face as she whispered, "Yes."

She prayed silently. And then she said, "You know I'm not a member of a church."

"Would you like for me to have one of our ministers come and talk with you about that?"

"Oh, yes, I'd love that."

She joined the church by profession of faith on Sabbath and died on Sunday.

"Let the sufferer be pointed to the One who is willing to save all that come to Him in faith. Earnestly, tenderly strive to help the soul that is hovering between life and death."—*The Ministry of Healing,* p. 120.

Suicide or Christ

Several patients attempted suicide during the time that I was with the clinic. The doctors asked me to work with them, and I found them very receptive to Christ and His love.

Every one of these individuals had two things in common. First, they felt that no one loved or cared for them. They had no one to whom they could safely turn. And second, they had problems in their lives that they could not resolve and did not know how to resolve, which made their situation seem hopeless.

And of course we have the solution to both problems— Christ. He loves with an "everlasting love," and He can deliver them "out of all their troubles." Jer. 31:3; Ps. 34:17.

I would like to share one of our experiences in helping this type of patient.

Jean was a fragile girl with "Dresden-doll" beauty. She had black hair, velvety white skin, deep bluish-purple eyes, and long lashes. She was born in eastern Canada and brought up by rigid Catholic parents. Her father was very abusive to her, making her stand in the snow for long periods of time without shoes or sometimes nailing her in the woodbox and leaving her for hours.

It is no wonder that to escape this situation she ran away when she was fourteen and married the first man who asked.

Unfortunately, she did not better her circumstances. The man she married was twenty years older than she. He was an alcoholic. When he drank, he beat Jean and their children. She had one child after another until she was so physically exhausted after the birth of her last child that she became acutely ill. For two months she fought for her life. The baby died.

In her weakened condition, very ill herself, she had failed to have her baby baptized. The priest came to their home and, discovering that the baby had not been baptized, harangued her for two hours for her negligence. He told her that she would never see her baby again, that the baby was in "limbo," that it was all her fault, that God would hold her responsible— and on and on.

All this was miserable enough to endure. But then her husband came home drunk and beat her and the boys. Ill, bruised, bereaved of her baby, and feeling a terrible responsibility for its lack of baptism, she felt she couldn't go on. There was no one to turn to for help. God wouldn't listen now. No one cared for her. There seemed to be no solution.

She went to the bathroom and got a bottle of sleeping pills and swallowed them all. Then she looked at her four boys and wondered, "What will happen to them? No mother. An alcoholic father!" The full impact of what she had done struck her. How could she abandon these four little boys?

She ran for the telephone book and hurriedly turned to the yellow pages under "physicians." She ran her finger down the column, not knowing whom to call. She dialed the number of the physician whose name her finger "accidentally" stopped on, she said.

But was it an accident that she dialed our clinic? And was it an accident that the doctor she asked for, who usually had that day off, had come in for some errand only a few moments before?

She was rushed to the hospital, and her life was saved.

Later, the doctor asked her, "Jean, how could you do such a thing?" She then unfolded the sad story of her life and how no one really loved her or cared.

"Well, that's where you're wrong," the doctor told her. "God loves you!"

And Jean replied, "Don't give me that stuff! How could a God of love take a little innocent baby and put it in limbo forever just because I was too ill to know what was going on?"

"I don't know where you got all your information about God and what He does. But it's certainly not a very accurate source. I'll tell you what," the doctor suggested. "I'd like to send our visiting nurse up to see you. Maybe she can help you understand what God is really like."

That's how I got acquainted with Jean. As we studied from week to week, it was just like seeing a wilted plant that has been given water. She simply came to life!

I couldn't keep up with all her questions and all the lessons she wanted to study. She was like a sponge soaking up water—she was so thirsty for knowledge. What a joy it was to see her begin to comprehend what God is like!

It was not long until she attended church with me one Sabbath. She told me that a warm feeling seemed to fill her. She felt a peace that she had never experienced before. It was the first time she had ever been inside a Protestant church. She attended evangelistic meetings with me and was later baptized.

There are so many lonely people, crushed by the blows of life and weighted down with problems too big for them. The only solution, the only escape, it seems to them, is suicide.

But thank God, there is an alternative. It's Christ!

And Then the Harvest

It was difficult, when Don was transferred to southern California, to terminate my work with the East Rose Medical Clinic. I did it very reluctantly. The fifteen months I worked for the clinic were the happiest and most rewarding months of my life.

My own relationship with Christ was enlivened as I had this opportunity to walk with Him and work with Him every day. It is a tremendous thrill to see the Holy Spirit working in the lives of men and women, to see the joy these people experience as they find Christ and learn to know and love Him. It's a satisfaction and fulfillment that you receive in no other way.

During those fifteen months at the clinic we saw twenty-five people make a decision for Christ. Twenty-three of these were either baptized or taken into the church on profession of faith. These were the ones I had worked with personally. Twenty-one other requests for studies came in from people in other conferences as a response to bookrack literature that had somehow reached them. We mailed these back to the fields from which they came so that they could receive personal attention. I don't know the results of those contacts, of course.

Many of the patients I studied with are still studying, and some are now preparing for baptism. The clinic presently has a nurse and a part-time Bible instructor to help with the interest.

I don't take any personal credit for the decisions that were made. Only the Holy Spirit can bring about conviction and conversion. I only tried to be where the need was and make literature and studies available—and let the Holy Spirit communicate the love of Christ through me. The results are His, not mine. He says, "Without me ye can do nothing." I was reminded of my weakness many times. But I also witnessed His strength. And it was the most rewarding experience I have ever known!

Another reason I can take no personal credit is that this was definitely a team project. Doctors, nurses, and office personnel all worked together, and we were all mutually interested in the progress of each patient. We can only thank the Lord for letting us be a channel—and give Him all the glory!

Helps for Soul Winners

Compiled by Marjorie V. Gray, RN

GOD'S CALL TO NURSES

"Many can be reached only through acts of disinterested kindness. Their physical wants must first be relieved. As they see evidence of our unselfish love, it will be easier for them to believe in the love of Christ. *Missionary nurses* are best qualified for this work."—*Counsels on Health,* p. 391.

"There are many lines of work to be carried forward by the *missionary nurse.* There are opportunities for well-trained nurses to go into homes and there endeavor to awaken an interest in the truth."—*Ibid.,* p. 388.

"Every medical practitioner may through faith in Christ have in his possession a cure of the highest value—a remedy for the sin-sick soul. . . . Through the sanctification of the truth God gives to physicians and *nurses* wisdom and skill in treating the sick, and this work is opening the fast-closed door to many hearts."—*Ibid.,* p. 331.

"The Lord wants wise men and women, who can act in the capacity of *nurses,* to comfort and help the sick and suffering. O that all who are afflicted might be ministered to by Christian physicians and *nurses* who could help them to place their weary, pain-racked bodies in the care of the Great Healer, in faith looking to Him for restoration!"—*Ibid.,* p. 388.

"In almost every community there are large numbers who do not listen to the preaching of God's word or attend any religious service. If they are reached by the gospel, it must be carried to their homes. Often the relief of their physical needs is the only avenue by which they can be approached. *Missionary nurses* who care for the sick and relieve the distress of the poor will find many opportunities to pray with them, to read to them from God's word, and to speak of the Saviour. They can pray with and for the helpless ones who have not strength of will to control the appetites that passion has degraded. They can bring a ray of hope into the lives of the defeated and disheartened. Their unselfish love, manifested in acts of disinterested kindness, will make it easier for these suffering ones to believe in the love of Christ.

"Many have no faith in God and have lost confidence in man. But they appreciate acts of sympathy and helpfulness. As they see one with no inducement of earthly praise or compensation come into their homes, ministering to the sick, feeding the hungry, clothing the naked, comforting the sad, and tenderly pointing all to Him of whose love and pity the human worker is but the messenger—as they see this, their hearts are touched. Gratitude springs up. Faith is kindled. They see that God cares for them, and they are prepared to listen as His word is opened."—*The Ministry of Healing,* pp. 144, 145.

"Everywhere there is a tendency to substitute the work of organizations for individual effort. Human wisdom tends to consolidation, to centralization, to the building up of great churches and institutions. Multitudes leave to institutions and organizations the work of benevolence; they excuse themselves from contact with the world, and their hearts grow cold. They become self-absorbed and unimpressible. Love for God and man dies out of the soul.

"Christ commits to His followers an individual work—a work that *cannot* be done *by proxy.* Ministry to the sick and the poor, the giving of the gospel to the lost, is not to be left to committees or organized charities. Individual responsibility, individual effort, personal sacrifice, is the requirement of the gospel."—*Ibid.,* p. 147.

"To every one who becomes a partaker of His grace the Lord appoints a work for others. Individually we are to stand in our lot and place, saying 'Here am I; send me.' Upon the minister of the word, the *missionary nurse,* the Christian physician, the individual Christian, whether he be merchant or farmer, professional man or mechanic—the responsibility rests upon all. It is our work to reveal to men the gospel of their salvation. Every enterprise in which we engage should be a means to this end. Those who take up their appointed work will not only be a blessing to others, but they will themselves be blessed."—*Ibid.,* p. 148.

SECRETS OF SUCCESS

"Without me ye can do nothing."
John 15:5

"The most earnest and continued efforts to acquire qualifications for usefulness are necessary; but unless God works with the human efforts, nothing can be accomplished. Christ says, 'Without Me ye can do nothing.' Divine grace is the great element of saving power; without it all human efforts are unavailing."—*Testimonies,* vol. 5, p. 583.

"It is not the capabilities you now possess or ever will have that will give you success. It is that which the Lord can do for you. We need to have far less confidence in what man can do and far more confidence in what God can do for every believing soul. He longs to have you reach after Him by faith. He longs to have you *expect great things from Him.* He longs to give you understanding in temporal as well as in spiritual matters. He can sharpen the intellect. He can give tact and skill. Put your talents into the work, ask God for wisdom, and it will be given you."—*Christ's Object Lessons,* p. 146.

"In this work all the angels of heaven are ready to co-operate. All the resources of heaven are at the command of those who are seeking to save the lost. Angels will help you reach the most careless and the most hardened."—*Ibid.,* p. 197.

"Remember that the Lord Jesus is the Master Worker. He waters the seed sown. He puts into your minds words that will reach hearts."—*Testimonies,* vol. 9, p. 41.

NEVER THINK OF FAILURE: "Workers for Christ are *never to think, much less to speak, of failure* in their work. The Lord Jesus is our efficiency in all things; His Spirit is to be our inspiration; and as we place ourselves in His hands, to be channels of light, our means of doing good will never be exhausted. We may draw upon His fulness, and receive of that grace which has no limit."—*Gospel Workers,* p. 19.

"When we give ourselves wholly to God and in our work follow His directions, He makes Himself responsible for its accomplishment. He would not have us conjecture as to the success of our honest endeavors. *Not once should we even think of failure.* We are to co-operate with One who knows no failure."—*Christ's Object Lessons,* p. 363.

LEAVE THE RESULTS WITH GOD: "The good seed may for a time lie unnoticed in a cold, selfish, worldly heart, giving no evidence that it has taken root; but afterward, as the Spirit of God breathes on the soul, the hidden seed springs up, and at last bears fruit to the glory of God. In our lifework we know not which shall prosper, this or that. This is not a question for us to settle. We are to do our work, *and leave the results with God.*"—*Christ's Object Lessons,* p. 65.

CHRIST'S METHOD BRINGS FRUIT: "Christ's method alone will give true success in reaching the people. The Saviour mingled with men as one who desired their good. He showed His sympathy for them, ministered to their needs, and won their confidence. Then He bade them, 'Follow Me.'

"There is need of coming close to the people by personal effort. . . . The poor are to be relieved, the sick cared for, the sorrowing and the bereaved comforted, the ignorant instructed, the inexperienced counseled. We are to weep with those that weep, and rejoice with those that rejoice. Accompanied by the power of persuasion, the power of prayer, the power of the love of God, this work will not, *cannot, be without fruit.*"—*The Ministry of Healing,* pp. 143, 144.

THE WORKER'S RESPONSIBILITY FOR SUCCESS

PERSONAL CONSECRATION: "If you are truly consecrated, God will, through your instrumentality, bring into the truth others whom He can use as channels to convey light to many that are groping in darkness."—*Testimonies,* vol. 7, p. 63.

"To everyone who offers himself to the Lord for service, withholding nothing, is given power for the attainment of measureless results."—*Ibid.,* p. 30.

"Those who consecrate body, soul, and spirit to God, will constantly receive a new endowment of physical, mental, and spiritual power. The inexhaustible supplies of heaven are at their command. . . . Through co-operation with Christ, they are made complete in Him, and in their human weakness they are enabled to do the deeds of Omnipotence."—*Gospel Workers,* pp. 112, 113.

"There is no limit to the usefulness of one who, by putting self aside, makes room for the working of the Holy Spirit upon his heart, and lives a life wholly consecrated to God."—*The Desire of Ages,* pp. 250, 251.

STUDY OF THE BIBLE: Source of Power: "It is a sin for those who attempt to teach the Word to others to be themselves neglectful of its study."—*Gospel Workers,* p. 249.

"The life of God, which gives life to the world, is in His word. It was by His word that Jesus healed disease and cast out demons. By His word He stilled the sea and raised the dead; and the people bore witness that His word was with power. He spoke the word of God as He had spoken it to all the Old Testament writers. The whole Bible is a manifestation of Christ. *It is our only source of power."—Ibid.,* p. 250.

PRAYER: "God's messengers must tarry long with Him, if they would have success in their work."—*Ibid.,* p. 255.

"It is only at the altar of God that we can kindle our tapers with divine fire."—*Ibid.,* p. 255.

"Prayer is the breath of the soul. It is the secret of spiritual power."—*Ibid.,* p. 254.

"Those who teach and preach the most effectively are those who wait humbly upon God, and watch hungrily for His guidance and His grace. Watch, pray, work—this is the Christian's watchword."—*Ibid.,* p. 257.

FAITH: "The greatest victories . . . for the cause of God . . . are gained . . . when with earnest, agonizing faith men lay hold upon the mighty arm of power. True faith and true prayer—

how strong they are!"—*Ibid.,* p. 259.

"This is the victory that overcometh the world, even our faith." 1 John 5:4.

"The worker for God needs strong faith. . . . The strength of those who, in faith, love and serve God, will be renewed day by day. . . .

"There is to be no despondency in connection with God's service. The faith of the consecrated worker is to stand every test brought upon it. . . .

"Jesus does not call on us to follow Him, and then forsake us. . . . *Whatever may be our situation, we have a Guide to direct our way."*—*Ibid.,* pp. 262, 263.

NEED: **Energy, Tact, Courage, Diligence, Industry, Willingness, and Love:** "Some who engage in missionary service are weak, nerveless, spiritless, easily discouraged. They lack push. They have not those positive traits of character that give power to do something—the spirit and energy that kindle enthusiasm. Those who would win success must be courageous and hopeful. . . . We must have *moral backbone,* and *integrity* that cannot be *flattered, bribed,* or *terrified."*—*Ibid.,* pp. 290, 291.

"Success depends not so much on talent as on *energy and willingness.* It is not the possession of splendid talents that enables us to render acceptable service, but the conscientious performance of daily duties, the contented spirit, the unaffected, sincere interest in the welfare of others."—*Christian Service,* p. 264.

"Many who are qualified to do excellent work accomplish little because they attempt little. . . .

"Remember that in whatever position you may serve you are revealing motive, developing character. Whatever your work, do it with exactness, with diligence; overcome the inclination to seek an easy task. . . .

"Christ gave no stinted service. He did not measure His work by hours. His time, His heart, His soul and strength, were given to labor for the benefit of humanity. Through weary days He toiled, and through long nights He bent in prayer for grace and endurance that He might do a larger work. . . . To His workers He says, 'I have given you an example, that ye should do as I have done.' " John 13:15.—*Gospel Workers,* pp. 291-293.

"Today I say to every worker for the Master, 'Courage in the Lord!' . . .

"Some look always at the objectionable and discouraging features, and therefore discouragement overtakes them. They forget that the heavenly universe is waiting to make them agencies of blessing to the world; and that the Lord Jesus is a never-failing storehouse from which human beings may draw strength and courage."—*Ibid.,* p. 265.

"If a man has tact, industry, and enthusiasm, he will make a success of temporal business, and the same qualities, consecrated to the work of God, will prove even doubly efficient; for divine power will be combined with human effort."—*Testimonies,* vol. 5, p. 276.

"Whatsoever is done out of pure love, be it ever so little or contemptible in the sight of men, is wholly fruitful; for God regards more with how much love one worketh than the amount he doeth."—*Ibid.,* vol. 2, p. 135.

"In choosing men and women for His service, God does not ask whether they possess learning or eloquence or worldly wealth. He asks: 'Do they walk in such humility that I can teach them My way? Can I put My words into their lips? Will they represent Me?—*Ibid.,* vol. 7, p. 144.

"Lift up Jesus, you that teach the people, lift Him up in sermon, in song, in prayer. Let all your powers be directed to pointing souls, confused, bewildered, lost, to 'the Lamb of God.' "—*Gospel Workers,* p. 160.

"Without a living faith in Christ as a personal Saviour, it is impossible to make your faith felt in a skeptical world. If you would draw sinners out of the swift-running current, your own feet must not stand on slippery places."—*Ibid.,* p. 274.

"I am instructed to say to my fellow workers: If you would have the rich treasures of heaven, you must hold secret communion with God. Unless you do this, your soul will be as destitute of the Holy Spirit as were the hills of Gilboa of dew and rain. When you hurry from one thing to another, when you have so much to do that you cannot take time to talk with God, how can you expect power in your work? . . .

"Commune with your own heart, and then commune with God. Unless you do this, your efforts will be fruitless, made thus by unsanctified hurry and confusion."—*Testimonies,* vol. 7, p. 251.

REWARDS OF SERVICE

PRESENT REWARDS: "Those who labor for the good of others are working in union with the heavenly angels. They have their constant companionship, their unceasing ministry. Angels of light and power are ever near to protect, to comfort, to heal, to instruct, to inspire. The highest education, the truest culture, the most exalted service possible to human beings in this world are theirs."—*Testimonies,* vol. 6, pp. 307, 308.

"In fellowship with God, with Christ, and with holy angels

they are surrounded with a heavenly atmosphere, an atmosphere that brings health to the body, vigor to the intellect, and joy to the soul."—*Ibid.,* p. 306.

"The pleasure of doing good to others imparts a glow to the feelings which flashes through the nerves, quickens the circulation of the blood, and induces mental and physical health."—*Ibid.,* vol. 4, p. 56.

"Nothing is drudgery to the one who submits to the will of God. 'Doing it unto the Lord' is a thought that throws a charm over whatever work God gives him to do."—*Ibid.,* vol. 9, p. 150.

"Those who give their lives to Christlike ministry know the meaning of true happiness."—*Ibid.,* p. 42.

"In doing for others, a sweet satisfaction will be experienced, an inward peace which will be a sufficient reward."—*Ibid.,* vol. 2, p. 132.

FUTURE REWARDS: "When the redeemed stand before God, precious souls will respond to their names who are there because of the faithful, patient efforts put forth in their behalf. . . . Thus those who in this world have been laborers together with God will receive their reward."—*Ibid.,* vol. 8, pp. 196, 197.

"What rejoicing there will be as these redeemed ones meet those who have had a burden in their behalf! . . . How their hearts will thrill with satisfaction!"—*Ibid.,* vol. 6, p. 312.

"The redeemed will meet and recognize those whose attention they have directed to the uplifted Saviour. What blessed converse they will have with these souls! 'I was a sinner,' it will be said, 'without God and without hope in the world, and you came to me, and drew my attention to the precious Saviour as my only hope.' . . .

" 'You read to me the precious promises of God's word. You inspired in me faith that He would save me. My heart was softened, subdued, broken, as I contemplated the sacrifice which Christ had made for me.' "—*Ibid.,* pp. 311, 312.

Christ will add His commendation: "I was sick, and ye visited me." Matt. 25:36.

"They that sow in tears shall reap in joy. He that goeth forth and weepeth, bearing precious seed, shall doubtless come again with rejoicing, bringing his sheaves with him." Ps. 126:5, 6.

"The fruit of the righteous is a tree of life; and he that winneth souls is wise." Prov. 11:30.

"And they that be wise shall shine as the brightness of the firmament; and they that turn many to righteousness as the stars for ever and ever." Daniel 12:3.

TOOLS FOR YOUR WORK

1. Bible small enough to carry in your purse or pocket
2. Notebook for your study guides
3. Notebook for your master file
4. Small notebook for messages
5. Literature box
6. Lesson box
7. Medical box
8. Shorthand pad for schedules
9. Red marking pen
10. Map of area to be covered
11. Crews's booklet

KEEPING THE DOCTORS POSTED

1. It is extremely important to report to the doctors any interest shown by patients, how studies are going, and

medical information from patients. The doctor is investing much in the program and likes to know what is going on. Be enthusiastic in reporting; your encouragement and good reports help the doctor feel that he is a part in witnessing and sharing Christ.

2. Drop by the clinic each day and ask for names the doctor may have for you to visit or names gathered by the clinic staff for you.

3. When you have someone ready for baptism, tell the doctor or other clinic personnel who are acquainted with the patient so that they can be at the baptism. It is nice to have the baptizing minister ask the doctor to stand during the patient's baptism, showing his part in the conversion.

4. Be certain you leave any messages from the patients with the nurse for the doctor or tell him yourself. Keep your notebook in your purse so you will have the messages with you. It is also useful for writing any names the doctor or personnel may give you.

METHODS OF SECURING AND PROMOTING INTEREST

1. *Doctors' Bookrack in Waiting Room*
   A. Keep filled with latest and best books.
   B. Make certain all books have card in back with return address of clinic.
   C. Use books from rack in your visitation in homes and hospital.

2. *Medical Personnel in Clinic*
   A. From the doctor's own suggestions as he recognizes needs of patient.
   B. From nurses in clinic.

C. From other personnel in clinic.

3. *Clinical Filed Correspondence (authorized)*

   A. Letters offering free study guides and Bibles to those interested.

   B. Visiting nurse can use this means of getting studies also.

4. *Hospital Rounds*

   A. Visiting patients to have surgery or attempted suicides or those having other illnesses. Leave literature and have prayer with. Use H F O R T. (Explained in section entitled "Leading a Person to Christ.")

   B. Follow up patients as they go home.

5. *House Calls*

   A. Injections, blood pressure treatments, etc—anything for reason to build interest.

   B. Leave literature from clinic each time.

6. *"Signs of the Times" or "These Times" Names*

   If the clinic has mailed *Signs* or other literature to certain patients, work on these names.

7. *Five-Day Plan to Stop Smoking or Cooking Schools or Diet Clinics*

   These people will be good ones to try to interest in studies.

8. *Conference Office*

   Check if names from your clinic requested free Bible and study guides and visit these names.

9. *"It Is Written," "The Voice Of Prophecy," "Faith For Today," "This Is Your World," etc.*

   Any patients viewing these programs would be excellent to visit.

Dear Patient:

No doubt you are well aware of the turmoil and confusion in the world at the present time. It seems that everywhere one looks he sees problems that have no solution. Man seems incapable of solving his own problems. The more he struggles with them the deeper he sinks into hopeless despair.

We here at the clinic believe there is a solution to these difficulties which face us today. We believe that the Bible holds the answers to man's most perplexing problems.

A television friend of ours has recently introduced a novel new way of studying and understanding the Bible. We are enclosing a brochure which describes this free offer we are making to all of our patients. After reading this pamphlet, if you are interested, please mail the enclosed card. Our visiting nurse will be happy to deliver your free Bible and acquaint you with this plan by which you can study and understand the Bible in your own home.

Sincerely yours,

TIPS ON VISITING HOSPITALIZED PATIENTS

1. Get quick history of patient from physician or chart—diagnosis, prognosis, religion, occupation, age, etc.
2. Do not make call during visiting hours.
3. Make calls brief, and let patient know the doctor sent you, "the visiting nurse."
4. Be friendly, helpful, interested in how patient feels; talk about his family, his occupation, religious background.
5. Listen to the patient, what he is saying. Don't talk about yourself.
6. Don't preach, lecture, or advise!

7. Don't be stiff and formal. A little humor helps break the ice.
8. Don't be an authority on illness; talk in generalities.
9. Don't act shocked at anything a patient may say or tell you.
10. Call back if not convenient for the patient at the time.
11. Say a little prayer before visiting each patient, asking that the Holy Spirit will help you to say the right thing and keep from saying the wrong things.
12. Be kind, gentle, understanding, and tolerant in all situations.
13. Never argue about anything with the patient.
14. Always leave a very small pamphlet or booklet from the clinic for the patient to read on faith or prayer or love, etc.
15. Don't ask the patient if you may have prayer with him; just say casually, "If you don't mind, I'd love to have a word of prayer with you before I run that God will give you a good day today."
16. Do try to "zero" in on the patient's needs. Be observant. Watch for openings that the Holy Spirit will give you to say a word about Christ's love and goodness or to witness by giving your testimony.
17. Don't try to give the appearance that you are a Bible worker—you are a visiting nurse, but you also have a deep concern for the spiritual well-being of the patient.
18. Keep your Bible in your purse, unless you are using it at the moment. We are to be wise as serpents!
19. Pat the patient's shoulder or hand or shake his hand to give that personal touch. There is nothing like the personal touch to show that you care.

49

TIPS ON VISITING IN THE HOME

1. Try to organize your calls into sections, or territories, so you can contact all in one area at the same time.
2. Same tips as in hospital visitation.
3. Ask the Holy Spirit to go with you at the beginning of each day.
4. Make a prayer list and lift each person by name before God's throne daily.
5. Find out when the people are home and note it on the master file.
6. Make up a master file book with the names and addresses and pertinent information to be kept with you in your car at all times.
7. If patient is busy or has company, excuse yourself and call back later.
8. Make these calls brief also.
9. After becoming acquainted, try to do little things like sharing a good recipe, some nice fruit, a loaf of homemade bread, etc.
10. If there are children, try to take some small books from the clinic or *Our Little Friends,* etc., to them.
11. Let the patient know your call is a free service of the clinic if you are there to give a treatment or take blood pressure, etc. Only charge for medication if injection is given.
12. Watch for any complications or things you notice that the doctor should be told about, and record them in a little notebook so you won't forget to tell him later.
13. Do not tell one patient about the problems of another patient. They must trust you, or you will not be able to gain their confidence.

14. Don't try to advise about how to raise children, etc.
15. Don't take sides in family arguments and problems.
16. Don't talk too much.
17. Don't act rushed and harried.
18. Don't overstay your welcome. (They will think your time isn't worth much.)
19. Don't give the impression that you are there to cram religion down their throats.

EASY METHOD OF GIVING BIBLE STUDIES

Advantages of the Gift Bible Method

1. The gift Bible plan, using the pagination system, makes it possible for the student quickly and easily to find the answers from the Bible itself, comparing scripture with scripture. As the student reads the answers from the Bible, his faith is strengthened and confidence in our message is increased.

   "God designs that men shall not decide from impulse, but from weight of evidence, carefully comparing scripture with scripture."—*The Desire of Ages,* p. 458.

2. Nurses can quickly and effectively learn to use this simple method of Bible study in a very short period of time.

3. By using this method of study, the student actually goes over the material three times:
   A. He reads the answers from the Bible.
   B. He writes the answers he has read.
   C. He repeats the answers to the visiting nurse.
   Thus, we have used the three avenues of learning recommended by many psychologists who

believe that we retain 10 percent of what we read, 30 percent of what we read and write, and 90 percent of what we read, write, and repeat. The percentage of retention of Bible facts greatly increases by this plan of Bible study.

4. Another advantage of this plan is the opportunity to become acquainted with the student by the personal contact and discussions.

"Your success will not depend so much upon your knowledge and accomplishments, as upon your ability to find your way to the heart. *By being social and coming close to the people,* you may turn the current of their thoughts more readily than by the most able discourse. The presentation of Christ in the family, by the fireside, and in small gatherings in private houses, is often more successful in winning souls to Jesus than are sermons delivered in the open air, to the moving throng, or even in halls or churches."— *Gospel Workers,* p. 193.

5. This method helps the student learn how to study the Bible in a systematic way on his own and acquaints him with the Bible, thus cultivating a love for the Scriptures.

How to Get Started

1. If possible, attend a class in New Testament witnessing where an experienced soul winner briefs you in the technique of sharing Christ with others.

2. Each nurse should have her own gift Bible and set of lessons. She should study the lessons and fill in the

answers so she will be familiar with the material she is to review with the student. She should check her answers and make certain they are correct.

3. Pray earnestly for heavenly wisdom and divine guidance as you go to your studies.

> "In working for perishing souls, you have the companionship of angels. Thousands upon thousands, and ten thousand times ten thousand angels are waiting to co-operate with members of our churches in communicating the light that God has generously given, that a people may be prepared for the coming of Christ."—*Testimonies,* vol. 9, p. 129.

> "In this work all the angels of heaven are ready to co-operate. All the resources of heaven are at the command of those who are seeking to save the lost. Angels will help you to reach the most careless and the most hardened."—*Christ's Object Lessons,* p. 197.

At the Patient's Home

1. Visit a little with the patients before you start your studies. Give them time to tell you what is on their heart so your study will not be constantly interrupted by little things they forgot about or want to pass on to you.

2. You might say the first time, "How did the lessons go? Did you enjoy them? Did you learn anything new?"

3. Take out your notebook of lessons and your Bible from your purse and say, "Perhaps we could go over

these more quickly if I read the questions and you read your answers, and we'll see if our answers match; OK?"

4. When the student has the lessons and is ready to start, say, "If you don't mind, I'd like to say a short prayer before we begin." Just say a one- or two-sentence prayer asking the Holy Spirit to guide in the study.

5. Don't pose as an authority on the Bible; be a "learner" with the student so he will relax and be at ease with you.

6. Briefly comment on the opening illustration and then read the first question, letting the patient read back the answer.

   A. If the answer is right, compliment the student for good work.

   B. Make a few comments as needed if you feel it will strengthen a point.

   C. Move right on through the lesson in this manner.

   D. Do not get too involved or make the lesson too complicated.

   "Jesus did not use long and difficult words in His discourses, He used plain language, adapted to the minds of the common people. He went no farther into the subject He was expounding than they were able to follow Him."—*Gospel Workers,* p. 169.

   "The greatest Teacher the world has ever known was the most definite, simple, and practical in His instruction."—*Ibid.,* p. 50.

7. If the student gives a wrong answer, don't say, "That's wrong." Say in a very kind way, "We seem to

have different thoughts on that question. Let's read that text again to be sure what the Bible says." Let the student turn to the text in the Bible and then you read the question again and let him read the Bible text. Usually he will see the right answer immediately.

    A. If the student does not fully understand a subject, leave a booklet on the subject. Never argue; let the silent witness do what argument will not do.

8. When you come to the end of the lesson, note the appeal questions and ask for the student's reaction to them in his own words. It is important that we get the student to make a decision on each subject presented so that he will be gradually moving forward in his acceptance of truth. If he is not ready to make these decisions, do not press the issue. In your closing prayer ask God to help the student in his understanding of this subject.

9. Keep the study moving right along. Don't let the student get sidetracked. Keep him on the subject you are studying at the time. If he asks about jewelry, makeup, the Sabbath, etc., just say, "That subject is coming in a later lesson, and I don't want to spoil your study before we get to it." This will help to avoid discussing controversial topics before the student has sufficient background to understand them or to accept them.

10. Always grade the student's lessons as "Excellent" or "Very Good." This encourages the student, and it is true even if he misses many of the questions. It is

excellent that he studied and very good that he is trying.

11. If you are asked a question you can't answer about the lesson you are studying, don't be embarrassed. Even the most profound scholars cannot answer every question! Just say, "I've never thought of that in just that way. I'll try to find the Bible answer and bring you the text or answer next week." Or, you might say, "I'm not certain what the answer to that question is, but I'll try to find it in my concordance and bring it to you when I come next week."

"There are many things beyond the comprehension of finite beings."—*The Ministry of Healing,* p. 431.

A. When you have a question on a particular subject and you have to look up the answer, write this down on that particular study so you will have the text or answer the next time a student asks you. Before long you will have most of the questions that people will ask written down on your lesson sheets.

B. Never try to answer a question if you don't know the answer. You'll find yourself in an embarrassing position, and you will lose the student's confidence in you.

12. Never preach, sermonize, or advise the student. Don't give the impression that you are "holier than thou." Let him know you are also human. Let him know that you also make mistakes, but with the Lord's help you are striving for perfection. Be humble and tenderhearted.

13. Follow the order of the lessons and go faithfully each week to study with the student. When he finishes the 24 lessons, start him on the advanced lessons. Always leave two to four lessons each week, depending on the student's ability to study thoroughly the lessons and the time he may have to study. If you leave too few, he may lose interest. Too many may discourage him.

14. Never condemn or act shocked at the behaviour or sinful practices of the student.

"It was a continual pain to Christ to be brought into contact with enmity, depravity, and impurity; but never did He utter one expression to show that His sensibilities were shocked or His refined tastes offended. Whatever the evil habits, the strong prejudices, or the overbearing passions of human beings, He met them all with pitying tenderness. As we partake of His Spirit, we shall regard all men as brethren, with similar temptations and trials, often falling and struggling to rise again, battling with discouragements and difficulties, craving sympathy and help. Then we shall meet them in such a way as not to discourage or repel them, but to awaken hope in their hearts. . . .

"It is always humiliating to have one's errors pointed out. None should make the experience more bitter by needless censure. No one was ever reclaimed by reproach; but many have thus been repelled and have been led to steel their hearts against conviction. A tender spirit, a gentle, winning deportment, may save the erring and hide a multitude of sins."—*The Ministry of Healing,* pp. 165, 166.

15. In order to succeed in this work we must have the power and presence of the Holy Spirit. We can only have this as we spend time in study of the Scriptures and communion with Christ.

"Without a living faith in Christ as a personal Saviour, it is impossible to make your faith felt in a skeptical world. If you would draw sinners out of the swift-running current, your own feet must not stand on slippery places."—*Gospel Workers,* p. 274.

"It is a sin for those who attempt to teach the Word to others to be themselves neglectful of its study."—*Ibid.,* p. 249.

Christ said, "Without me ye can do nothing." John 15:5.

16. Be optimistic. Never think or talk of failure. God is responsible for the results when we do our best.

"When we give ourselves wholly to God and in our work follow His directions, He makes Himself responsible for its accomplishment. He would not have us conjecture as to the success of our honest endeavors. Not once should we even think of failure. We are to co-operate with One who knows no failure."—*Christ's Object Lessons,* p. 363.

"Workers for Christ are never to think, much less to speak, of failure in their work. The Lord Jesus is our efficiency in all things; His Spirit is to be our inspiration; and as we place ourselves in His hands, to be channels of light, our means of doing good will never be exhausted. We may draw upon His fulness, and receive of that grace which has no limit."—*Gospel Workers,* p. 19.

17. Keep your pastor posted on the progress of the student and take him with you so the student can become acquainted with him on a personal basis. It will help the pastor when the time comes for him to prepare the student for baptism.

PRESENTING CHRIST

1. As the student progresses in his study, he will show more enthusiasm each week you study with him. What a thrill it will be to see the opening of the student's mind and heart to the influence of the Holy Spirit.

2. Your main objective is to lead this person to accept Christ as his Saviour. When you have laid the foundation of knowledge that is necessary and have studied enough so that the student knows what the plan of salvation is, give the student the gospel presentation (sample in back of book), asking the student to receive Christ as his Saviour and Lord.

3. This invitation to accept Christ as Saviour and Lord should be given before the Sabbath and other testing truths are studied if possible. When the heart is surrendered to Christ and the person is willing to let Christ lead him, it becomes easy for him to accept the special truths that we have to share with the world.

4. As soon as you have studied the Sabbath, ask the student to visit church with you sometime. Invite him home for

dinner and show him how enjoyable the Sabbath can be when we have the Lord of the Sabbath in our hearts and homes. If there are evangelistic meetings being held in the area, invite the student to attend with you. (Sample letter of invitation is in back of book.)

LEADING A PERSON TO CHRIST

I like the New Testament witnessing technique of leading a person to make a decision for Christ.

I do not feel it is fair to ask a person to accept Christ and follow Him if he hasn't sufficient knowledge to make an intelligent decision. How can you accept someone and something that you do not understand? What is he accepting if he has not studied the life of Christ or His plan of salvation? I feel it is best to study with the student until he is familiar with the Bible teachings on the origin of sin, man's fall, the plan of redemption, and conversion. If a person has this knowledge, then the following outline will be easy to present and understandable to the patient. However, I would never try to lead a person to Christ the first time I met him unless he was seriously ill and not expected to live. It is important to gain friendship and confidence before talking about a personal commitment. The first visit I use the HFORT. H=talking about the person't health or physical condition; F=talking about the family; O=talking about occupation. (Sometimes that was all I talked about on the first visit and left the other two until the next visit.) R=talking about religious background; and T=my testimony—what Christ has done for me and how He has changed my life.

When leading a person to Christ, you can use the following questions or some similar to them.

1. Have you come to the place in your experience that you have the assurance of eternal life?
   I recently discovered that you can have this assurance. 1 John 5:13.
2. What do you think the requirements for eternal life are? (Usually they will say, "go to church," "give money," "be good to your neighbor," "keep the commandments," etc.)

I know that I have good news for you. You know, I used to think that I had to do something to earn eternal life. I thought that I had to do a few more good things than bad things, but then I discovered that eternal life is a *free gift* from God.

Rom. 6:23; Eph. 2:8.

Isn't it wonderful that we don't have to earn salvation or deserve eternal life? God gives us this wonderful gift because He loves us!

John 3:16.

You see, His love was so great for us that He gave His only Son to save us from eternal death. In fact, He doesn't want any of us to be lost.

2 Peter 3:9.

He isn't willing that any should perish. God wants every person that has ever lived to be saved regardless of race or station in life.

God doesn't want to see us die, so He said He was willing to take our sins to save us from suffering and death.

Rom. 3:23.

You see, we don't deserve this kind of treatment because all of us are sinners. Every person alive today has disobeyed God. In verse 10 it says, "There is none righteous, no, not one." In fact, the Bible tells me that all of my righteousness is as filthy rags. Isa. 64:6. My good works will not deliver me from my past sins and mistakes.

Rom. 5:12.

Now, I discovered something else. You see, every one of us who has disobeyed God and sinned is doomed to death!

This situation calls for God's grace. He loves us and doesn't want to see any of us perish; but, at the same time, all of us have sinned and are doomed to die. How could God save us and give us eternal life?

There was only one way God could do this, and that was to give of Himself. He was willing to take the sinner's punishment so that the sinner might get credit for Christ's perfect life.

Jesus stepped forward and volunteered to take the punishment of the sinner so that the sinner could be given the eternal life that Christ deserved. You understand that Christ was more than a perfect created being, don't you? You will remember what the Bible says (in *John 1:1-3):* "In the beginning was the Word, . . . and the Word was God."

You see, Jesus was God. So it was God who, in the form of the Son, took our place and died for our sins on the cross of Calvary. Let's read about this sacrifice in Isa. 53:4, 5. [Describe the sacrifice made.] What happens to our sins? Verse 6. "The Lord hath laid on him [Christ] the iniquity of us all." You see, God the Father in His great love took your sins and punishment and put them on Christ as He hung on the cross. It was not the nails in His hands or feet that killed Him. He died of a broken heart, because our sins separated Him from His Father and He could not stand this separation.

What a tremendous realization! It was my sins—the many things that I have done contrary to God's will and His law—that made it necessary for Christ to die. My sins broke

His heart. When we realize this in its fullness, it will lead us to repentance as it did the people on the Day of Pentecost. Peter had just spoken to the people about their responsibility in the death of Christ. Notice what happened. *Acts 2:37, 38.*

Peter said "repent." Repentance is a deep sorrow for the sins that we have committed. It is such a deep sorrow that we are determined to turn from the sins that killed our Lord and Saviour. Would you willingly continue to do anything that would be responsible for the death of one whom you love dearly? A mother backed her car over her little daughter in the driveway. Could that mother ever drive a car in a careless manner again after this experience without realizing what her carelessness had done to one that she loved so much?

Now, the question comes, How can I be certain of receiving this gift? There is only one way that you can have it. By *faith!* Eph. 2:8, 9. Now faith is more than just a mental assent to certain facts. It is more than believing that there is a supreme being in heaven and that Jesus died 1900 years ago. The Bible tells us in James 2:19, "The devils believe, and tremble." Does this save the devils? No! More knowledge on their part that God exists and that Christ died on the cross would not bring a change in their life, nor would it forgive them for their sins!

True faith in Christ is accepting His sacrifice and trusting Him completely as our Saviour from sin. Faith is the hand by which we reach out to accept the gift of eternal life that God is reaching down to give us. All we need to do is trust Jesus completely, receive Him fully, and give Him control of our lives. Here is an envelope of Bible lessons. When do these lessons become yours? When you believe that I will give them and you reach out and take them. So it is with God's gift of salvation. We must reach out and take it if it is to be ours!

63

Does this make sense to you?

(Yes.)

Would you like to reach out by faith and accept this wonderful gift that God reaches down to give you in His Son?

(Yes.)

Now, let's make certain that you realize what is involved in this decision.

1. Trust in Jesus alone for forgiveness. It isn't what you can do but what Christ has done for you on the cross.

2. You do want to repent and turn from your sins for which Christ died?

3. How can you do this? How can you live the life that Christ invites you to live? By trusting Him to come into your life and live out His life in you. He did not sin. He was victorious. If He lives in your life and controls you, He will help you live for Him. He wants to come into your heart. *Rev. 3:20.*

   Don't you want Him to come in and control your life so that you can follow Him?

TEXTS FOR SPECIFIC SITUATIONS

[Write on flyleaves of Bible]

When Ill and in Need of Healing

Heb. 4:15—Jesus is "touched with the feeling of our infirmities."

James 5:16—We are told to "pray one for another, that ye may be healed."

Ex. 15:26—The Lord said, "I am the Lord that healeth thee."

Matt. 4:23—Christ healed "all manner of sickness and all manner of disease."

Ps. 103:3, 13, 14—The Lord "healeth all thy diseases."

Some conditions of healing:

Luke 8:48—"Thy faith hath made thee whole."

Mark 9:29—"Prayer and fasting" can produce healing.

1 Cor. 12:28—One of the gifts of the church is healing.

James 5:14, 15—"Call for the elders. . . : and the prayer of faith shall save the sick."

Deut. 7:11-15—Keep the commandments, and the Lord will take away all sickness.

Luke 22:42—We should be willing to let God decide— "not my will."

2 Cor. 12:9—Paul was refused healing and was told, "My grace is sufficient for thee."

Heb. 5:8—Jesus "learned . . . obedience by things which he suffered."

When Afraid or Fearful

Ps. 4:8—"I will both lay me down in peace, and sleep."

Ps. 34:7—"The angel of the Lord encampeth round about them."

Heb. 13:5, 6—"I will never leave thee, nor forsake thee. . . . I will not fear."

Ps. 91:10, 11—"There shall no evil befall thee. . . . For he shall give his angels charge over thee, to keep thee in all thy ways."

Ps. 23, 91, 121. (These chapters are marvelous in allaying fear.)

Promises to the Backslider

Jer. 3:22—"Return, ye backsliding children, and I will heal your backslidings."

Isa. 55:7—"Let him return unto the Lord, and he will have mercy upon him; . . . for he will abundantly pardon."

Hosea 14:2-4—Christ will heal our backsliding.

Luke 15:7—More joy in heaven over one that returns than over ninety-nine saved persons.

Ps. 37:31—Keep law in heart, and none of our steps will slide.

Luke 15:24—Joy and rejoicing when the prodigal son returns.

Hope for Bereaved or Dying (Adapt to specific case)

Matt. 5:4—"Blessed are they that mourn: for they shall be comforted."

Rom. 8:28—"And we know that all things work together for good."

Luke 22:42—"Not my will, but thine, be done."

2 Tim. 4:6-8—Paul said "I am now ready to be offered, . . . I have fought a good fight, . . . I have kept the faith: . . . there is laid up for me a crown of righteousness."

Acts. 20:24—Paul again says, "But none of these things move me, neither count I my life dear unto myself."

Comforting thoughts of the resurrection:

John 11:21-25—Christ's promise of resurrection to Martha.

1 Thess. 4:13-18—Promise of resurrection at second coming.

1 Cor. 15:51-57—Victory over the grave. (John 5:28, 29.)

1 Cor. 15:19-26—Hope for the dead.

Jer. 31:16—"They shall come again from the land of the enemy."

Isa. 64:17-19—"I create new heavens and a new earth. . . . The voice of weeping shall be no more." (Verses 21-25.)

Rev. 21:4, 5—All tears wiped away; no more sorrow or death.

Isa. 65:21-25—"Mine elect shall long enjoy the work of their hands."

(Psalm 23.)

God's Love for Us

1 John 4:8, 16—"God is love."

John 3:16—"For God so loved the world."

Jer. 31:3—"I have loved thee with an everlasting love."

Rom. 8:38, 39—Nothing can separate us from the love of God.

Matt. 5:45—He gives blessings to both the good and the bad.

1 John 3:1—"What manner of love . . . we should be called the sons of God."

1 John 4:7-11—"Herein is love."

Eph. 2:4-6—"He loved us, even when we were dead in sins."

Rev. 1:5, 6—"Unto him that loved us, and washed us from our sins."

Worried, Troubled, Having Difficulties

Prov. 3:5, 6—"Trust in the Lord with all thine heart."

Ps. 46:1—"God is our refuge and strength, a very present help in trouble."

Isa. 43:2—I will be with thee through water and fire.

Rom. 8:28—"All things work together for good."

Ps. 37:39, 40—He is "strength in time of trouble."

Ps. 55:22—"Cast thy burden upon the Lord." (See also 1 Peter 5:7.)

Ps. 34:17—"The righteous cry, and the Lord heareth, and delivereth them out of all their troubles."

Ps. 119:71—"It is good for me that I have been afflicted; that I might learn thy statutes."

John 16:33—"Be of good cheer."

Ps. 91, Ps. 34, Ps. 103.

Financial Problems

Isa. 41:17—He will not forsake the poor.

Ps. 109:31—He shall stand at right hand of the poor.

Ps. 37:3-5—"Trust in the Lord . . . ; and . . . thou shalt be fed."

Ps. 37:25—Have "not seen the righteous forsaken, nor his seed begging bread."

Phil. 4:19—"My God shall supply all your need."

Matt. 6:25-34—"Seek ye first the kingdom of God . . . ; and all these things shall be added."

1 Peter 5:7—"Casting all your care upon him; for he careth for you."

Matt. 7:11—"If ye . . . give good gifts unto your children, how much more shall your Father . . . give . . . good things to them that ask him?"

How to Receive Forgiveness

God knows our sins:

Heb. 4:13—"All things are naked and opened unto the eyes of him."

Eccl. 12:14—"God shall bring every work into judgment, with every secret thing."

What are we to do?

    Num. 5:6, 7—"Confess their sin which they have done."

    Prov. 28:13—Confess and forsake sins.

Promises of forgiveness:

    Isa. 1:18—"Though your sins be as scarlet, they shall be as white as snow."

    1 John 1:9—"If we confess our sins, he is faithful and just to forgive us our sins."

    Micah 7:18, 19—God will pardon. He delights in mercy. He will have compassion.

    Isa. 55:7—"He will abundantly pardon."

    Eph. 4:32—Forgive others, even as God has forgiven you.

    Mark 11:26—"If ye do not forgive, neither will your Father which is in heaven forgive your trespasses."

If Persecuted After Accepting Christ

    Matt. 5:10-12—"Blessed are they which are persecuted for righteousness' sake."

    Rom. 12:14—"Bless them which persecute you."

    Heb. 11:24-40—Stories of those who have suffered for Christ.

    Mark 10:29, 30—Anyone suffering for Christ's sake will receive a hundredfold and eternal life in world to come.

    Ps. 9:9—"The Lord . . . will be a refuge for the oppressed."

    Isa. 43:2—"When thou passest through the waters, I will be with thee."

    Ps. 34:19—"Many are the afflictions of the righteous: but the Lord delivereth him out of them all."

1 Peter 4:12, 13—"Rejoice inasmuch as ye are partakers of Christ's sufferings."

Rev. 2:10—"Fear none of these things . . . : be thou faithful unto death, and I will give thee a crown of life."

Answered Prayer

Matt. 7:7-11—"Ask, and it shall be given you."

Ps. 37:7—"Wait patiently."

Luke 18:1—Be persistent.

Heb. 11:6—Be earnest.

Mark 11:24—Belief is necessary. (James 1:6, 7.)

Mark 9:24—"Help thou mine unbelief."

1 John 5:14, 15—"Ask . . . according to his will."

Ps. 66:18, Isa. 59:1, 2—Will not hear if we cherish sin.

Phil. 4:6—Mingle prayers with thanks.

John 14:13, 14—Ask in Christ's name.

2 Cor. 12:8, 9—Not every prayer will be answered Yes. (Experience of Paul asking for healing.)

Good Angels (Angel means messenger)

Number of good angels:

Rev. 5:11—"Ten thousand times ten thousand, and thousands of thousands."

Heb. 12:22—"Innumerable company of angels."

Their work:

1 Peter 3:21, 22—Subject to Christ. (Heb. 1:6.)

Heb. 1:14—Minister to heirs of salvation.

Matt. 18:10—Each child of God has accompanying angel.

Ps. 34:7—Protect those that fear God. (Ps. 91:10-12.)

Dan. 6:22—Protected Daniel.

Ps. 103:20—Excel in strength.

Matt. 16:27; Matt. 24:31—Will accompany Christ at His coming.

GOSPEL PRESENTATION
HOW TO LEAD A PERSON TO CHRIST

Introduction:

You need to prepare the person for a presentation of the gospel. Your friendliness and interest in him will do much to put him at ease and will help you in presenting Christ to him. The following steps will help:

Health—Find out about the patient's physical condition.

Family—Ask patient about family. Set him talking about loved ones.

Occupation—Learn about what the prospect does. This will help you know about his interests and when you can visit in the future.

Religion—Ask about religious background. This will let you get a glimpse of religious thinking.

Testimony—The best way to lead into the message that you have come to share is by a word of testimony.

We would suggest the following order to prepare the prospect for prayer.

Qualifying questions:

"Mr._____, may I ask you a very important question? Have you come to the place in your experience that you have the assurance of eternal life?"

If the answer is negative, say, "You know, I think that I have good news for you, but before I tell you about it, let me ask you another question.

"If in the judgment day, God should ask you, 'Why should I let you into My heaven?' what would you say?"

After he answers, say "Let me be certain that I understand what you mean before I go any farther."

When you understand his thinking, continue. "I said before that I thought I had good news for you. After what you have just said, I know that what I am about to share with you is the best news that you have ever heard. I used to believe just like you do. When I was a child, my Sunday School teacher taught me that if I were very good I would someday be able to go to heaven and have eternal life.

"As I began to understand the gospel better, I found out that eternal life is free. The Bible tells us: 'The wages of sin is death; but the gift of God is eternal life.' How much do you expect to pay for a gift? Now, notice: It says that *the gift of God is eternal life.*

"In fact, God tells us that we cannot earn eternal life. In Eph. 2:8, 9, we read: 'For by grace are ye saved through faith; and that not of yourselves: it is the gift of God: not of works, lest any man should boast.' You see, it isn't something good that we can do in the future which will earn forgiveness for our past sins. Heaven is not earned or deserved.

"Most people think that by reading their Bibles, going to church, practicing the golden rule, or keeping the commandments they will be able to spend eternity with God; but that is not correct.

"Now, the problem man faces is that he is a sinner. We have all sinned and come short of the glory of God. In fact, the Bible describes man's true condition in pretty graphic terms. Romans 3:10-12 says: 'As it is written, There is none righteous, no, not one: there is none that understandeth, there is none that seeketh after God. They are all gone out of the way, they are together become unprofitable; there is none that doeth good, no, not one.' The Bible teaches that all of us have sinned. You can see that, can't you?

"Notice that our sins have separated us from God and eternal life. Not a one of us is good enough to get into heaven, because God's standard is perfection. Jesus says that we have to be perfect: 'Be ye therefore perfect, even as your Father which is in heaven is perfect.'

"I was thinking the other day that if I committed just three sins a day, in sixty years I would have over 65,000 sins charged to my account. No wonder we have to be saved by God's grace. 'By grace are ye saved through faith; *and that not of yourselves.'*

"The problem a man faces in trying to save himself becomes even more acute when we read what the Bible says about God. We know that God is loving and merciful, as He says in 1 John 4:8. 2 Peter 3:9 says, He is 'not willing that any should perish.'

"But God is also a God of justice. He says in Exodus 34:6, 7 that by no means can He clear the guilty. He doesn't want to punish man for his many sins, but His justice demands that He deal with sin.

"What is the answer to this dilemma? God was willing to send His own Son to this world to make eternal life available to sinful man.

"It's important to know just who Jesus Christ is. Many do not realize it, but Jesus is God. He is more than just a good man or a great healer or teacher. He was God in human flesh. 'In the beginning was the Word, and the Word was with God, and the Word was God. . . . And the Word was made flesh, and dwelt among us.' Thomas recognized this when he said to Jesus, 'My Lord and my God.'

"Why did He leave His heaven and come to this world? He did it to demonstrate God's great love for man, to show what a truly perfect life is. But, most of all, He came to give us eternal life. You will remember that the angel told Joseph, 'Thou shalt call his name JESUS: for he shall save his people from their sins.'

"You see, Jesus did not die because of any sins that He had done. The Bible says: 'All we like sheep have gone astray; we have turned every one to his own way; and the *Lord hath laid on him the iniquity of us all.*'

"We have discovered that all of us have sinned many times. Suppose that this book represents the record of all those sins. They weigh down on us and our conscience, and if in the judgment day they have not been taken away, we will be condemned. But, you see, the Bible says that even though we have sinned and gone astray, God has laid on Jesus the iniquity of us all. It was the guilt of all our sins that separated Jesus from His Father and broke His sacred heart. You see, God takes our sins and charges them to the account of Jesus.

"Notice it says that 'it pleased the Lord to bruise him.' He is 'smitten of God, and afflicted.' God poured out the punishment for our sins on His perfect Son.

"That is why in the judgment day God can be just and let us have eternal life. Jesus took our punishment, and we get credit for His perfect life of righteousness. All of this is free. It is a gift that God wants to give to every person. 'The gift of God is eternal life.' It is yours free.

"But how do we receive this gift? 'By grace are ye saved through *faith.*' You see, faith is the key that opens the door of heaven. Someone has said that faith is a beggar reaching out to accept a gift of a king. Let's make certain that we understand what this faith is, or perhaps we should first decide what it is not. It is not just mental assent to the existence of a supreme being. The Bible says that 'the devils . . . believe, and tremble.' Merely believing that Jesus lived and died 2000 years ago is not saving faith. Nor is it just trusting God for temporal blessings. Some people trust Jesus to keep them from dying when they are sick or they ask for food when hungry. Real faith is simply trusting Christ completely for our salvation. Christ didn't come to this earth and die just to keep us safe on a plane trip or help us get over an operation. He came to make sure that we are saved with Him for eternity.

"Faith is trusting Jesus Christ alone for our salvation. People can trust in only one of two things—in themselves and their good works, of in the sacrifice of Jesus. A real load was lifted off my shoulders when I realized that I could be certain of receiving eternal life by trusting fully in Jesus. He proved by His resurrection that His sacrifice had taken care of the sin problem.

"The Bible says: 'But as many as received him, to them gave he power to become the sons of God, even to them that believe on his name.' John 1:12.

"Someone has said that in salvation there is:

> Something to believe—
>> (That Jesus died for us.)
> Someone to receive—
>> (We must receive Him as our Saviour.)
> Something to become—
>> (As we let Him live in our heart,
>> He will help us become like Him.)

"We have not only accepted Him as our Saviour, but He now reigns in our heart as Lord of our life. Does that make sense to you?

"You have just heard the greatest story ever told about the greatest offer ever made by the greatest Person who ever lived.

"Now the question is: Do you want to receive this gift of eternal life that Christ left heaven and died on the cross to give you?"

(If the prospect indicates that he wishes to accept Christ, then you should clarify his commitment.)

"Let's make certain that you understand fully what is involved in this commitment of your life to Christ. First of all, you are going to trust in Christ alone for the forgiveness of every sin that you have ever committed, and you are going to receive Him as your Saviour. Is that right?

"Second, you now realize that it was your sins that caused His death on the cross. This will naturally lead you to repentance. You now realize that your sins caused the death of your dear Friend and Saviour. This realization makes you sorry for your sins, and you are determined that by His grace and with His help you are no longer going to do those things that were responsible for His death. If you knew you were doing something that was killing one of your loved ones, would you continue to do that thing if you really loved that person? How then can you continue to sin when you now realize that your disobedience to God in the past broke the heart of your Saviour?

"You will probably say just now, 'Well, that is all well and good. I don't want to do those things that are contrary to God's will, but where will I get the strength to overcome those sins?' You will remember that we decided that the only way that we could have forgiveness is through trusting in Jesus alone. Well, the only way that we can overcome is through trusting in Him alone for the power and strength to live for Him and with Him. Only as we allow Him to become the Lord of our life will we find the strength that we need to live the Christian life here on this earth. In our own strength we can never do it. We need to link our weakness with His strength. He wants to give us the strength and power that we need just now. He says, 'Behold, I stand at the door, and knock: if any man hear my voice . . . , I will come in and sup with him.' He wants entrance into our hearts so that He can now take control of our lives.

"You do want to receive Him as your Saviour and your Lord just now, don't you?

"If this is what you want to do, we can go to the Lord in prayer right now and tell Him about it."

Prayer

Assurance

John 6:47.

Backslidden Adventist or Outright Sinner

"Have you wished that you had the assurance that if you should die tonight you would spend eternity with the saved?

"What do you think will be God's entrance requirements for that eternal city? Who will be allowed to enter that city and live with Him throughout eternity?

The Professed Christian

"Have you come to the place in your relationship with

Christ where you really understand God's will for your life and that you are joyfully doing His will?

"You know, of course, that Christ said that it will be by the fruitage of our lives that the difference will be seen between the professed Christian and the one who has really surrendered his will and life to Christ. Notice what He said in Matthew 7:20-22: 'Wherefore by their fruits ye shall know them. Not every one that saith unto me, Lord, Lord, shall enter into the kingdom of heaven; but he that doeth the will of my Father which is in heaven. Many will say to me in that day, Lord, Lord, have we not prophesied in thy name? and in thy name have cast out devils? and in thy name done many wonderful works?'

"You see, our relationship to the will of God demonstrates whether or not Christ really rules in our life and heart. 1 John 2:3, 4 says: 'And hereby we do know that we know him, if we keep his commandments. He that saith, I know him, and keepeth not his commandments, is a liar, and the truth is not in him.'

"We demonstrate our love to God by our actions. In 1 John 5:1-3 we read: 'Whosoever believeth that Jesus is the Christ is born of God: and every one that loveth him that begat loveth him also that is begotten of him. By this we know that we love the children of God, when we love God, and keep his commandments. For this is the love of God, that we keep his commandments: and his commandments are not grievous.''

YOUR PERSONAL WITNESS

"Our confession of His faithfulness is Heaven's chosen agency for revealing Christ to the world. . . . That which will be most effectual is the testimony of our own experience. . . .

God desires that our praise shall ascend to Him, marked by our own individuality. These precious acknowledgments to the praise of the glory of His grace, when supported by a Christlike life, have an irresistible power that works for the salvation of souls."—*The Desire of Ages,* p. 347.

Some "Do's" in Preparing a Brief Testimony of Personal Experience

1. Do give the "wedded-witness" of your union with Christ. Rom. 7:4.
2. Do be prepared to tell others humbly but courageously, "I am a Christian."
3. Do keep your personal testimony brief—from two to four minutes.
4. Follow this brief outline: Living My Life at Its Best
   a. My life *before* surrendering to Christ.
   b. *How* I came to be a Christian. (Tell how it happened.)
   c. My life *since* becoming a Christian. (Tell of the change, joy, and blessings.)
5. Do use such phrases as (see *Testimonies,* vol. 8, p. 321):
   a. "I needed help, and I found it in Jesus."
   b. "I found the Bible to be the voice of God to my soul."
   c. "In Christ the hunger of my soul has been satisfied."
6. If you accepted Christ in your tender youth, do emphasize what this Christian heritage has done for your life.
7. Do start with an interest-arousing statement, and climax with Christ as the Author of salvation. Use one of your favorite scriptures.

Some "Don'ts" and Some Things to Avoid

1. Don't use our denominational jargon which fails to communicate properly. Avoid such phrases as "since I came into the message" or "after I accepted the truth." Keep your witness Christ-centered. It is better to uplift Christ as Saviour with such phrases as "since I accepted Christ" and "after I accepted Jesus as my personal Saviour." Remember, salvation is in Christ.

2. Don't glamorize sin by telling in detail how *wicked* you used to be.

3. Avoid being wordy. Keep your witness brief. The Lord loves those with a "contrite heart," and brevity gives others an opportunity to ask questions which are waiting for Bible answers.

4. Don't speak critically of other churches; all comments should be seasoned with love and tact.

Be Pleasant and Positive

1. Practice your personal witness for Christ until it becomes part of you.

2. Give your personal testimony in a clear, concise, and coherent manner.

3. Pray that your countenance will radiate Christian faith, and let your smiles speak the language of heaven.